Long and Orange

What Am I?

by Kathryn Camisa

Consultant: Eric Darton, Adjunct Faculty
New York University Urban Design and Architecture Studies Program
New York, New York

BEARPORT PUBLISHING

New York, New York

Credits
Cover, © Radoslaw Lecyk/Shutterstock; 2, © Syrist/Dreamstime; TOC, © Alexander Demyanenko/Shutterstock; 4–5, © Ian Sheppard/Alamy; 6–7, © Kris Wiktor/Shutterstock; 8–9, © Nadezda Zavitaeva/Shutterstock; 10–11, © Syrist/Dreamstime; 12–13, from the holdings of the Golden Gate Bridge, Highway and Transportation District; 14–15, © Pete Niesen/Shutterstock; 16–17, © robertharding/Alamy; 18–19, © Martin M303/Shutterstock; 20–21, © Martin M303/Shutterstock; 22, © holbox/Shutterstock; 23, © Radoslaw Lecyk/Shutterstock; 24, © prochasson frederic/Shutterstock.

Publisher: Kenn Goin
Senior Editor: Joyce Tavolacci
Creative Director: Spencer Brinker
Design: Debrah Kaiser
Photo Researcher: Thomas Persano

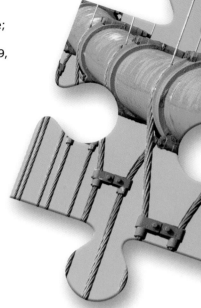

Library of Congress Cataloging-in-Publication Data

Names: Camisa, Kathryn, author.
Title: Long and orange : what am I? / by Kathryn Camisa.
Description: New York, New York : Bearport Publishing, [2018] | Series: American place puzzlers | Includes bibliographical references and index.
Identifiers: LCCN 2017039490 (print) | LCCN 2017042408 (ebook) | ISBN 9781684025381 (ebook) | ISBN 9781684024803 (library binding)
Subjects: LCSH: Golden Gate Bridge (San Francisco, Calif.)—Juvenile literature.
Classification: LCC TG25.S225 (ebook) | LCC TG25.S225 C36 2018 (print) | DDC 624.2/30979461—dc23
LC record available at https://lccn.loc.gov/2017039490

For more information, write to Bearport Publishing Company, Inc., 45 West 21st Street, Suite 3B, New York, New York 10010. Printed in the United States of America.

10 9 8 7 6 5 4 3 2 1

Contents

What Am I?

Every day, cars and trucks zoom across me.

4

I am painted
orange.

6

Look up!
I have two
huge towers.

Thick, strong cables help support me.

I have five horns.

They make loud sounds when it is foggy.

12

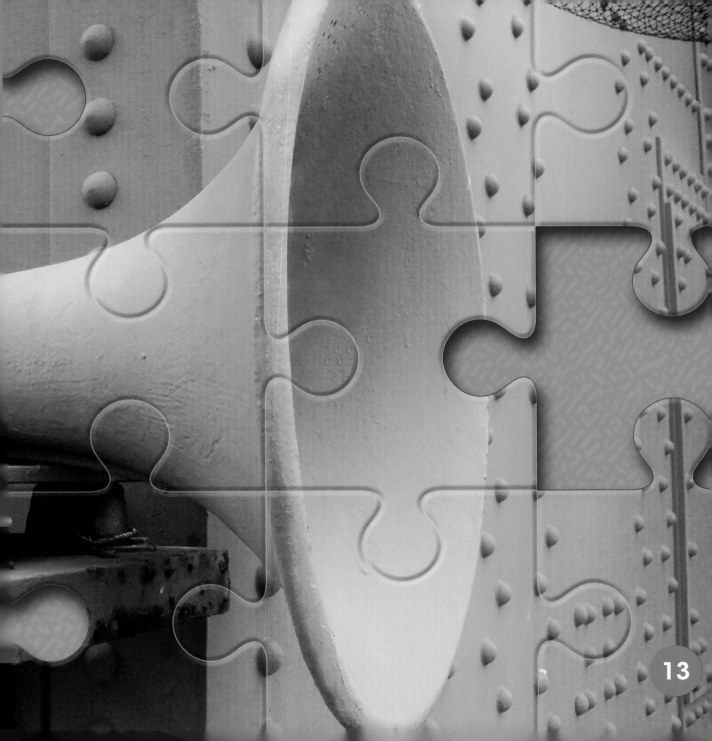

13

Water runs
underneath me.

14

Fog often covers me.

16

What am I?

Let's find out!

19

I am the Golden Gate Bridge!

21

Fast Facts

The Golden Gate Bridge is one of the world's most famous bridges. It was completed in 1937. When it first opened, people celebrated with parades and fireworks!

The Golden Gate Bridge

Height of Each Tower:	746 feet (227 m)
Total Length:	8,981 feet (2,737 m)
Width:	90 feet (27 m)
Length of Main Cables:	7,650 feet (2,332 m)
Cool Fact:	About 40 million vehicles travel across the Golden Gate Bridge each year!

Where Am I?

The Golden Gate Bridge is located in California. It connects the city of San Francisco to Marin County.

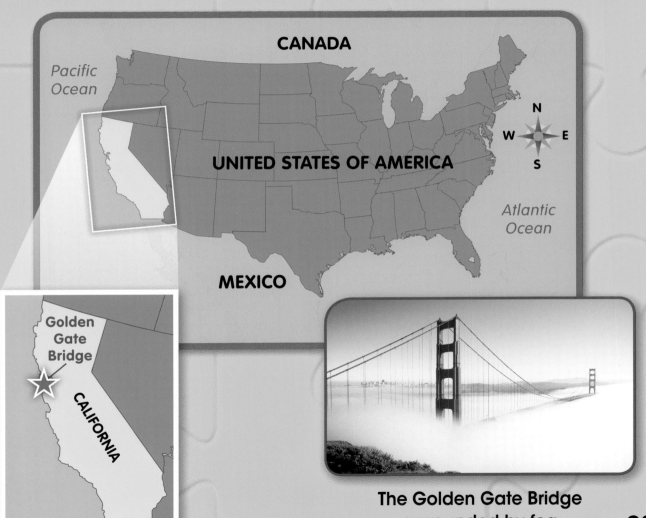

The Golden Gate Bridge surrounded by fog

Index

Read More

Olson, Elsie. *Building the Golden Gate Bridge (Engineering Marvels).* North Mankato, MN: Abdo (2017).

Zuehlke, Jeffrey. *The Golden Gate Bridge (Lightning Bolt Books: Famous Places).* Minneapolis, MN: Lerner (2009).

Learn More Online

To learn more about the Golden Gate Bridge, visit
www.bearportpublishing.com/AmericanPlacePuzzlers

About the Author

Kathryn Camisa lives far from the Golden Gate Bridge in New York City, where she works in children's publishing.

24